A ZEN BOOK OF HOURS

Frederick Franck

Codhill Press

New Paltz, New York

ISBN 1-930337-13-2

how wondrous!

I draw water!

I call this book "A Zen Book of Hours", for it came to me hour after hour in two days during which I hardly slept, ate or drank.

It started as I sat in my studio, feeling restless and empty, staring at a jar on my table, full of pencils and brushes, when my eye fell on a tiny square brush I once bought in Kyoto, years ago, but never used.

Suddenly, almost automatically, I dipped the little brush into my ink bottle and then watched it noting down something on a sheet of paper: a little image of a man drawing water from a well..."bottomless well" I thought.

This was the overture to this Book of Hours, for in the forty-eight hours that followed I could not stop jotting down words and images that were almost ideograms or hieroglyphs. They seemed to be dictated one after the other from somewhere deep inside me. The words that came welling up, at once turned themselves into those images, or perhaps it went the other way around, for I tend to think in images rather than concepts. But this was obsessive and would not stop, until the last of some hundred sheets of paper in my drawer was used up.

I was frightened. I had no idea what coerced me to do this. I did not even care whether I was jotting down the quotations correctly. But I was vaguely aware that what I scribbled and drew was a potpourri of fragments from decades of reflection on Mahayana Buddhist sutras and writings, and snatches of Gospel texts, often from the Prologue to Saint John's and the apocryphal Gospel of Thomas. They seemed to continue welling up irresistibly.

But why?

Then, suddenly, I shuddered and thought of the letter from England that came the day before. It was from Gerry, whom I had not seen since I left London for New York almost half a century ago. We kept on exchanging letters, often on spiritual, religious matters ever since. In this latest letter she mentioned some symptoms that bothered her lately. I answered it at once, begging her to see a doctor right away. Sometimes I had felt this correspondence to have become a burden, but I did not dare to put an end to it. It was Gerry's letter that ended it.

For just after I ran out of paper, there was a phone call from London. An old woman's voice asked:

"Are you Frederick Franck?" and when I confirmed it, she said that she was a friend of Gerry's whom she had promised to call me if anything should happen to her.

"Gerry, I am sorry having to tell you died suddenly. She went out to mail a letter on the corner and returning home, she collapsed ... a massive heart attack."

My Book of Hours had dictated itself as Gerry's Requiem.

Daisetz Teitaro Suzuki whose classical writings on Zen have accompanied me on my life's journey, wrote:

"The so called spiritual experience is no other than the experience of pain raised above mere sensation".

Bottomless Well
from which all rises, grows
and boundless Ocean
back into which it flows
          Angelus Silesius, 17th Century

The water that boils in the kettle
is drawn from the Well
that is bottomless
          Sen Rikyu, 14th Century Tea Master

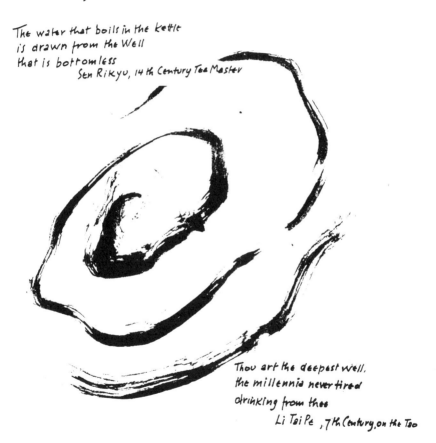

Thou art the deepest well,
the millennia never tired
drinking from thee
          Li Tai Pe , 7th Century, on the Tao

Zuizan used to call out to himself:
Zuizan!
"Yes, Master...," he answered.
Are you awake?
"Yes, Master..."
really awake?
"Yes, Master!!"
And won't you let yourself be deceived again?
"Never, Master, never!"

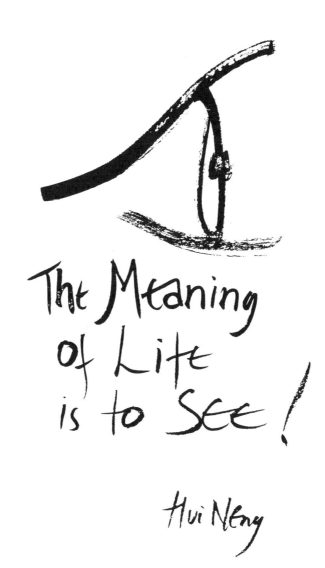

The Meaning
of Life
is to See!

Hui Neng

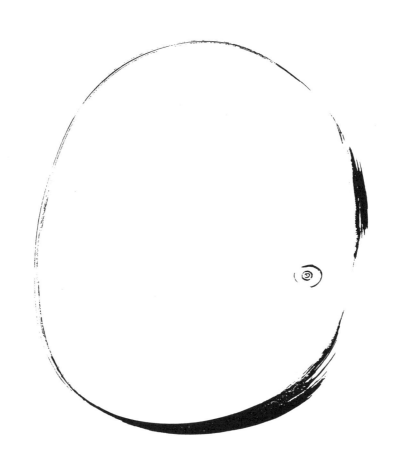

In the beginningless beginning
there was
the Meaning

What dwelleth here
I know not
but my heart is
full of awe
and the tears trickle down

When the Ten Thousand things
are seen in their Oneness, we return
to the Origins and remain where
we have always been
                              Sen T'sen

Solitary
naked body
in
the
midst
of the
10.000
things...

Keiji Nishitani

The Tao cannot be divided, it can be shared

Spiritual talk
makes a fine
cover
to sell a lie

Both the slayer
and the slain
are like dewdrops
thus to be regarded

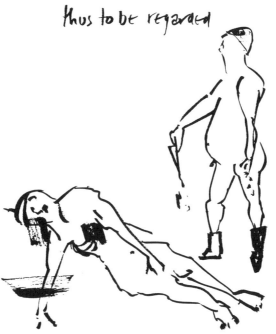

Summer grasses
all that remains
of the warrior's
dream

they have taken the wounds of
the people lightly... they say
peace, peace, where there is
ho peace...

Jeremiah 6.14

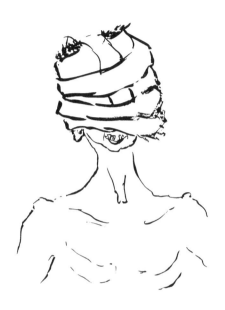

they do not see what they look at,

hence they know not what they do

standing.
going,
sitting,
whatever you have to do
and you are in the best place
to learn profound
meditation
          Bukko

Why do they call me a fool?
I wonder...

But how could I know
who doesn't even know
who I is!

Hanshan

Who are you?
I do not know, Your Majesty

the kingdom is within you
and without you

gospel acc. to Thomas

Master, you used to say: Mind is the Buddha,
   -Why do you say now: No mind, no Buddha?
   "I said Mind is the Buddha", to stop the baby crying..."
   And when the baby stopped crying?
   "No Mind, no Buddha!"

the clearsighted eye
turns the light back
to see
its own
Original Nature

The eye with which I see
God
is the same Eye with which
God
sees me

Meister Eckhart

He who seeks the Buddha outside of his own mind makes the Buddha into a devil   Dogen

It is like being immersed in the
great ocean, the waves over your
head, yet begging pitifully for
water

gensho

I set out to beg
my food
but spent my time
gathering violets
in the fields of Spring

Ryokan

If you want to do
a certain thing
you first have to become
a certain person

once you have become
that certain person
you will not care
anymore about
doing that certain thing

Dogen

the distance
between this pigeon's brain
and mine
is minute
compared to that
between mine
and Bodhi's
Wisdom
Compassion

does the dog
have the Buddha Nature?

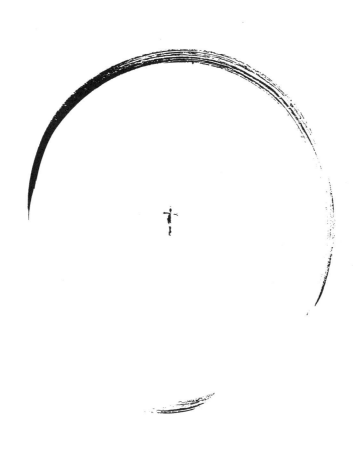

I and the Father are not-two

God
is
no
uncle,
God
is

On Earthquake!

Hasidic saying

all this universe
is in this eye
of mine!

SEPPO

Is there anything more miraculous
than the wonders of nature? the
monk exclaimed.
The Master said:
"Yes, your understanding, your awareness
of the wonders of nature."

The landscape you draw
is an internal landscape
emerging from the
formless, colorless
Ground of Being

Rinzai said.

' There is that True Man, without rank or label
in this mass of red flesh... He goes in and out of
your sense gates incessantly... Have you
seen this True Man?"

"But, Master, what is that True Man?.."

Speak! Speak!

Rinzai Roku

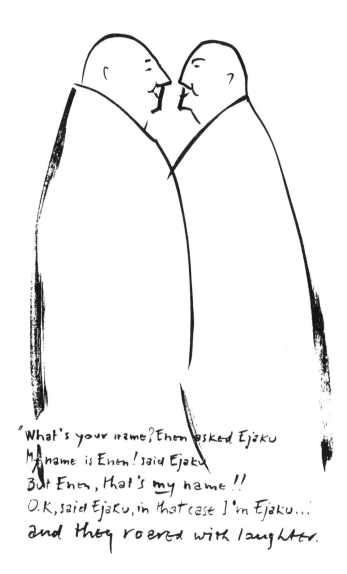

"What's your name? Enen asked Ejaku
My name is Enen! said Ejaku
But Enen, that's my name!!
O.K, said Ejaku, in that case I'm Ejaku...
and they roared with laughter.

If you still have to talk
about **Ultimate Reality**
see how it manifests itself
nakedly
in
every thing!

My short span of spring
how many years will it be?
Houchan

as to the skin
what a difference between
a man and a woman
but as to the bones:
born so human!

Ikkyu

sentient beings are
intrinsically Buddhas
It is like water and ice
without water ice can't exist
Hakuin

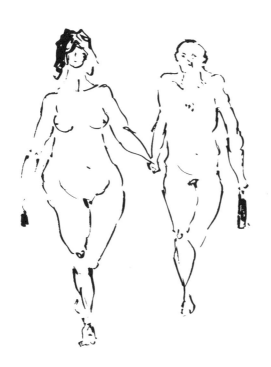

people walking?

Karma walking...

Buddha Nature walking...

Monks should do their zazen in their zendo
I, a knight, practice it on horseback

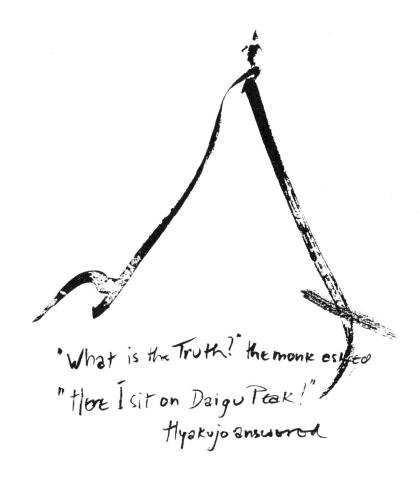

"What is the Truth?" the monk asked

"Here I sit on Daigu Peak!"
Hyakujo answered

The 10.000 Things and myself
are of one root

ZOZENRUN

the One embodies itself in the
multitude of things; does not stand
aloof from them

D.T SUZUKI

The religions ~~are~~
delusional constructs
formed around
an infallible core

Innumerable Buddhas
Enlightened...
innumerable Christs crucified...
always the same Christ, the same Buddha!

If Christ were born
a thousand times
in Galilee
it was all in vain
until he is born in thee.
        in me

AngHus Silesius

Anyone who pretends
he Knows God is depraved

St. Gregory Nanzianzan

if you say
"God Exists"
then act
as if
God exists.

do you believe
in God?

– Which One?

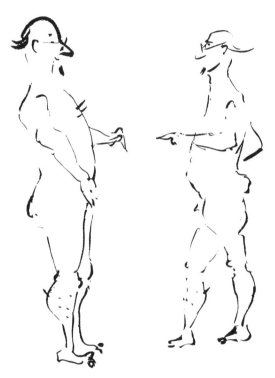

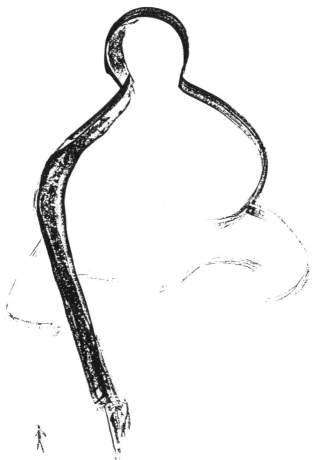

When a monk complained about the world's evil,
the Buddha stretched his hand towards the Earth:
"on this Earth I attained Liberation."

the Buddha Mind
is one
with my own Essence

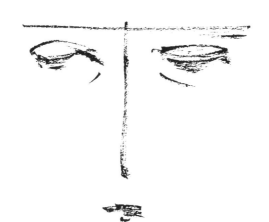

Show me your Original Face before you were born!

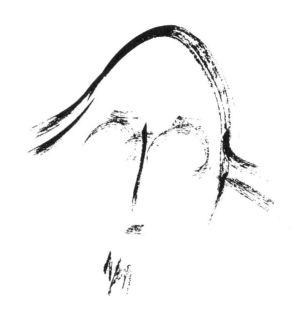

"What are you?"
I am no What!

I am only I...
in relation to you!

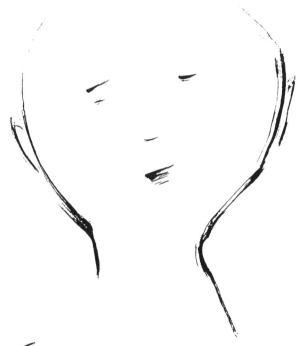

I am neither I
        nor Other,
both I and other...

"before Abraham was
I AM"

When the Christ says I :
it is the I of all the Masters :
the Way , the Truth ,
the Life

Christ has no body on earth,
no hands, no feet but yours

Theresa of Avilla

the grasses
whisper

'This
is
my
Body"

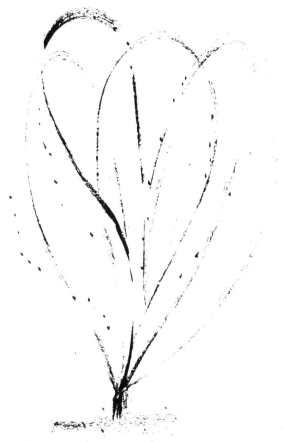

God is a fountain flowing into
Itself

Dionysius

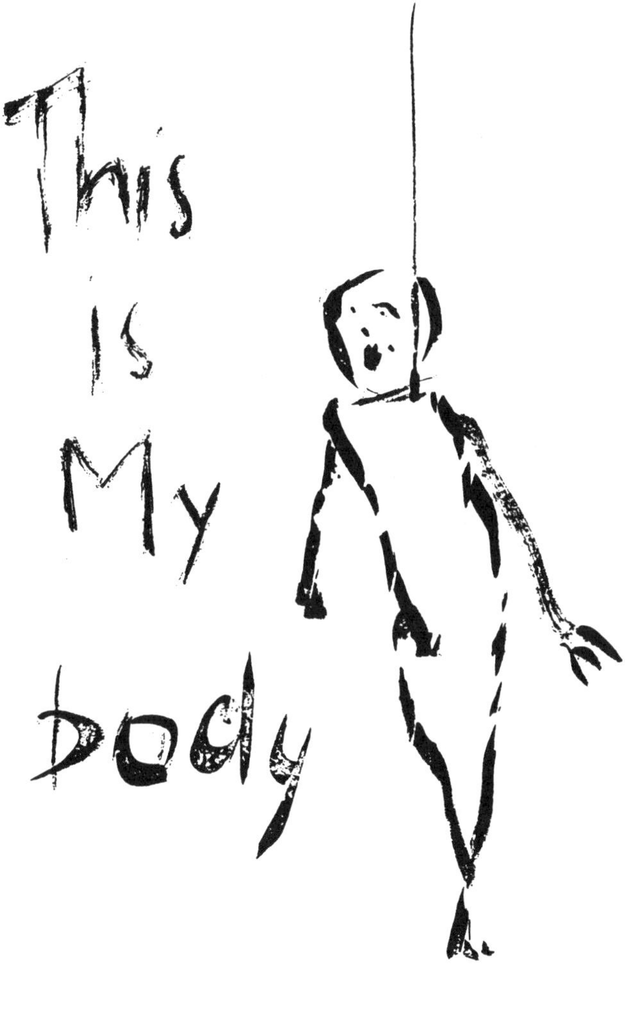
This is My body

from here all the Buddhas
all the Christs
Entered the World

Tia nun Myoei

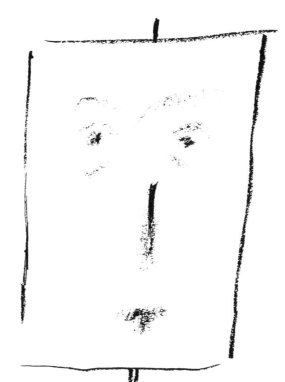

In all faces
is seen
the face of faces
veiled
as in a riddle

the nightingale
even before His Lordship
the same voice

Issa

the existent
and the non existent
are the same under
different names

LaoTsu

I meet him
he is no other than myself
yet I am not him..

Dosan

the infinitely small
is as large
as the infinitely big

Sengtsen

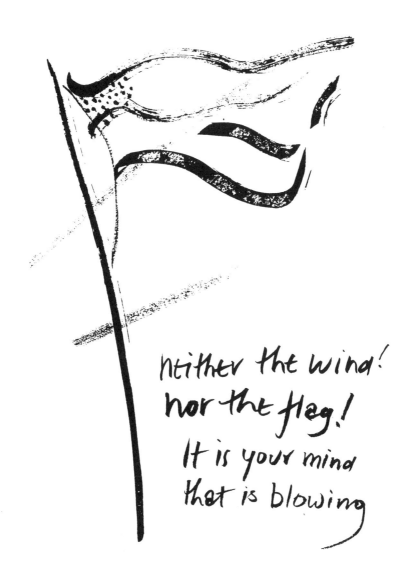

neither the wind!
nor the flag!
It is your mind
that is blowing

if you walk, walk!
if you sit, sit!
don't wobble
whatever you do
Ummon

the garden grasses
they fall
and lie as they fall

Ryokan

The Void is a living Void

pulsating in endless rhythms of creation
and destruction. The great Void does not
exist as Void, it embraces all
Being / non-Being

Holy?
nothing holy, Your Majesty!
all holy! Great Emptiness!

if a man sees the Tao
in the morning

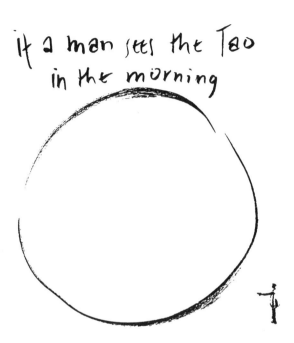

he may die in the evening
regretting nothing

Confucius

What do I bequeathe
as my legacy:
flowers of spring
cuckoos in summer
maple leaves of autumn

Ryokan

Where does the soul go
when the body dies?
It does not need to go
anywhere.
                Jakob Boehme

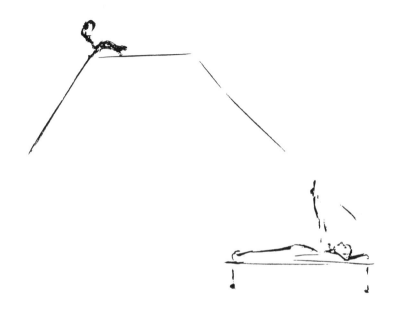

When Kukai lay dying, he heard
a squirrel screeching on the roof,
He bid his disciples listen,
_This is It, he said, and nothing more!

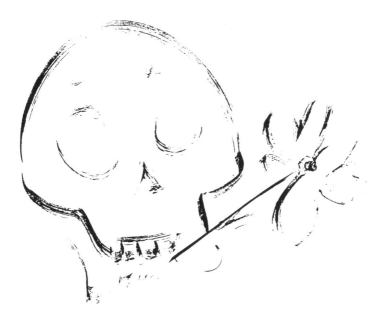

I shall not die
I shall not go anywhere
just don't ask me
any questions,
I shall not answer

Ikkyu

Let there be Light!
He said.

Who was the Eye witness?

Let there be dark!
We said

Who will be the eyewitness?

I am come as Time,
the waster of peoples
ready for the hour
that ripens their ruin

Upanishads

don't dismiss these
as verses
an old fellow
likes to scribble!
What I have in mind
is to arouse,
to open someone's eye
here or there.
The bright one will
see at a glance where
the arrow flies,
the dull will prattle
about rhythm
and rhyme.   Hakuin

The more you
look for it
the less you'll find it

yoka

Colophon
An edition of 500 copies
Written, drawn and designed by Frederick Franck
Printed by Warwick Press LLC, Warwick, N.Y.